Christian Unity —
The Next Step

'That They May All Be One'

FR. KEVIN E. MACKIN, OFM

WESTBOW
PRESS®
A DIVISION OF THOMAS NELSON
& ZONDERVAN

WestBow Press books may be ordered through booksellers or by contacting:

WestBow Press
A Division of Thomas Nelson & Zondervan
1663 Liberty Drive
Bloomington, IN 47403
www.westbowpress.com
1 (866) 928-1240

ISBN: 978-1-9736-8719-1 (sc)
ISBN: 978-1-9736-8718-4 (e)

Print information available on the last page.

WestBow Press rev. date: 03/17/2020

CONTENTS

Introduction

I am a "cradle Catholic" and have only gratitude about it. In my mid-century Brooklyn neighborhood, Marine Park to be precise, everyone seemed to know everyone else. Church and parochial school were integral to family life, and people generally associated with their community—other Catholics.

Not much changed in things Catholic from high school to college, as I prepared to become a Franciscan friar-priest. I began graduate classes in 1960 in Washington D.C., and four years later received a degree in sacred theology from Catholic University of America.

Little did I realize that the 1960s would be a decade of incredible change.

The October 1958 conclave of cardinals had elected Cardinal Angelo Roncalli, 76, as Pope John XXIII. He was a surprise pontiff, and in 1959, he astonished seventeen cardinals by announcing to them that he would convene an ecumenical council. Reactions varied from proverbial yawns to murmurings about what the curia was up to, and some were horrified, thinking no good would likely come of a council.

John XXIII's papal ministry was relatively brief, five years. Yet it was one of the most revolutionary times in the history of the Catholic Church. Good Pope John captured many minds and hearts with his affable personality. He desired to renew the life of the Church, to advocate for peace and social justice, and above all to reestablish Christian unity.

To do so, he read the signs of the times with a thesaurus view of Catholic: wide-ranging, extensive, all-embracing. What had been primarily a Protestant unity movement became, with Pope John's impetus, more globally Christian, at least among theologians. During the many years he had served among Orthodox Christians as an apostolic delegate in Bulgaria, Turkey and Greece, he realized that before we can discuss what divides us and how we can be united, we first have to get to know each other and treat separated Christians as brothers and sisters in the same spiritual family.

Pope John created a specific Secretariat for Promoting Christian Unity, directed by Cardinal Augustin Bea.

For nearly four hundred years after the sixteenth century Reformation, the Catholic and Protestant churches drew further and further apart. Diatribe generally described relations between the two.

In the nineteenth century, Protestant churches realized they were exporting to Africa, Asia and South America a divided and divisive Christianity. They were competing, duplicating resources, and often undermining one another. In 1910, many missionary societies came together in Edinburgh, Scotland to work out a common strategy. Thus was born the twentieth century ecumenical movement. Out of this conference came the International Missionary Council in 1921, Life and Work in 1925 (its slogan: "Doctrine divides; service unites") and Faith and Order in 1927.

The purpose of Faith and Order was to draw the churches together to explain their convictions to one another. The methodology up to 1952 was to compare ecclesiologies: some churches say this, others say that.

Nathan Soderblom's vision in Life and Work gave rise to the World Council of Churches, established in 1948, comprising the most significant churches except, notably, Roman Catholics.

The World Council sees itself as a "fellowship of churches which confess the Lord Jesus Christ as God and Savior according to the Scriptures, and therefore seeks to fulfill together their common calling to the glory of the one God, Father, Son and Holy Spirit."

The World Council does not see itself as a "super church" but as an instrument to serve the various churches. Its great task is to continue the work of Life and Work, Faith and Order, and the World Missionary Council by making cooperation between the churches easier and stimulating and strengthening ecumenical and missionary endeavors.

Although a number of Catholic movements, institutes and associations promoted Christian unity during the first half of the twentieth century, Catholic Christianity had officially entered the modern ecumenical movement very slowly.

Pope John XXIII began the first session of the Council in October 1962 and wrapped it up that December with scores of working documents sans promulgation. The Council was automatically suspended when the pope died on June 3, 1963. He was later declared a saint. When Cardinal Giovanni Montini, Archbishop of Milan, was elected Pope Paul VI on June 21, the unwieldy seventy-three schemata were re-drafted and reduced to seventeen, and the Council's pastoral nature was re-emphasized.

The second session of the Council ended December 4, 1963 with the promulgation of the *Constitution on the Sacred Liturgy*. The third session in 1964 brought the promulgation of the *Dogmatic Constitution on the Church (Lumen gentium)*, the *Decree on Ecumenism*, and the *Decree on the Eastern Churches*. The fourth and final session concluded December 8, 1965 with two more constitutions, six decrees and three declarations.

The 1964 *Decree on Ecumenism* emphasized the gifts of the Orthodox churches, whose power to govern themselves according to their own disciplines was recognized. Referring to the churches in the West, where more numerous differences exist, the Decree listed several points that all held in common, but it also declared that the separated brethren have not retained the authentic and full reality of the Eucharistic mystery.

Two principles regarding theological statements are important in ecumenical dialogue. The first is that all such statements must be understood in their historical context. The second is that no theological statement exhausts the fullness of truth.

Almost all the Protestant churches profess a belief in baptism and in Scripture as the word of God. Their celebration of the "Lord's Supper" is reverent, and their worship often retains elements that were conspicuous in ancient liturgies. Their charitable works often show an enormous Christian generosity.

There are generally three stages of ecumenical dialogue. The first, obviously indispensable, may be called "ecumenical initiation." This is simply getting genuinely acquainted with one another. An openness and willingness to meet others can be exciting and awkward. Frequently we do not quite know how to behave. Yet it's imperative to remember that acquaintance is only a beginning. Ecumenical initiation is only the first stage.

The second stage is "ecumenical cooperation." The obvious agenda includes experiments in common prayer, community service, and common work in education: primary, secondary, college and graduate levels. All of us, Catholics and Protestants, are responsible for the Christian education of our people in all its dimensions. Protestant/Roman Catholic cooperation in education at every level is still an unsettled frontier — a challenge for all Christians.

Christians must sooner or later raise the question of theological unity. So a third stage may be called "ecumenical negotiation." We must explore areas of agreement in our theological understandings. But we must also find and probe areas of difference—always in true Christian gentleness. The most obvious area is the study and interpretation of Scripture, as all Christians believe the Scriptures are a unique and indispensable source of revelation.

Another is the study of our common history as Christians: "longer, larger and richer than any of our separate histories in our divided churches." What we need, according to the Methodist theologian Albert Outler, is a historically honest answer to the question: How has the gospel been received, expressed and transmitted in the succeeding generations of the people of God? We need to study divisions which have occurred in the course of Christian history, to find a way beyond their divisiveness.

A crucial problem to consider is the future of "belief." Catholics and Protestants together must realize their common witness to the reality of the living God, and their common challenge is "unbelief." Every man or woman of faith has something to which they are ultimately committed. Christians have found the ultimate meaning of life in Jesus Christ—via an intensely personal God who comes in love to call all of us into communion and friendship with God and our fellow human beings.

Into this ecumenical world I entered as a newly minted Catholic priest, ordained in 1964. After pursuing a master's degree in religious education under the leadership of the renowned Gerard S. Sloyan at Catholic University of America, and another degree in history, and teaching in a Catholic high school and a minor seminary for one year each, I returned to CUA for a doctoral program in the ecumenical sphere: a fascinating venture for this "cradle Catholic" who as a youngster yearned to be a missionary.

My dissertation topic eventually became "In Search of the Authentic Christian Tradition." I did research in New York City at Union Theological Seminary and the National Council of the Churches of Christ; at the Perkins School of Theology at Southern Methodist University in Dallas, Texas where Albert Outler had a trove of materials;

and at the World Council of Churches library in Geneva, Switzerland.

I also corresponded with recognized theologians on the topic: for example, Georges Florovsky, the Orthodox Christian priest; Sydney Ahlstrom, a Lutheran specialist in religious history of the United States; Lutheran bishop Kristen Skydsgaard; Lukas Vischer, the Swiss Reformed church theologian; and Rev. Georges Tavard of the Augustinians of the Assumption.

This ecumenical study/experience was indeed an adventure, and it radically deepened my understanding of Christianity.

Now, after more than a half century of ministry as a Franciscan Catholic priest, I reflect on those ambitious times and studies and the central point of Christian life: "that they may all be one" (John 17:21). I am grateful to Janet Gianopoulos for helping me to assemble this summary plan.

Where is Christian unity today? And how best go forward in unity?

CATHOLIC CHRISTIANITY: A SURPRISE ENTRY INTO THE ECUMENICAL MOVEMENT

When Pope John XXIII sprung the idea of a Council on January 25, 1959 in the Basilica of St. Paul Outside the Walls, it caught Christendom by surprise. There were surprises from beginning to end. And still more in the aftermath.

The calling of a Council initially stirred negative feelings among many Protestants. When a Lutheran professor wrote an article suggesting that Protestants ought to reconsider their attitude toward Rome and the possibility of a converging union, others warned that Rome had been for centuries a kind of basilisk, a legendary reptile, fascinating and dangerous. And suddenly Rome was open to unity.

The charisma of John XXIII did much to counter this negative attitude. Many believed he was committing the Catholic Church to renewal.

He was in fact a staunch traditionalist in both polity

and belief. His *Journal of a Soul* confirms that, and also indicates his admirably direct self-examination.

Pope John wanted a more effective and up-to-date Church within the framework of the traditional Catholic Church. He assumed that if Rome were loving enough, many non-Roman Christians would return to their home. His basic ecumenical understanding in the beginning was "reunion by return." He wanted a new Pentecost.

Yet he wanted it without any significant discontinuity with the past in which he himself had grown up. Which reminded some of the minutes of a town council:

> Resolved: To build a jail;
> to utilize the materials of the old jail for the new;
> to use the old jail during the period of construction.

It was only natural for Pope John to turn over the arrangements for his Council, as with his other special projects, to the same people in the Roman curia. Their deepest conviction was to continue the Church as it was.

The curia staged a rehearsal for the ecumenical Council with a three-day Synod of Rome in 1960, in which many regulations of clergy in the diocese of Rome were addressed. These had been last revised in 1874. The Synod updated outmoded dress codes and general behavior. Nothing substantial changed. Pope John and the curia were quite pleased with the Synod and supposed that the process could be replicated in the Council for a safe aggiornamento.

Some seemed to have forgotten the strength of the

so-called immobilist presence in the Catholic Church for two hundred years beforehand.

One can't appreciate the breakthroughs in liturgical reform, ecclesiological self-understanding, religious freedom and ecumenical dialogue unless one is aware of this history of the Church. The more we understand that, the more Vatican II is seen as the end of one era and the opening of another.

Albert Outler, a Methodist observer at the Council and a key figure in the ecumenical movement, summarized the fortress mentality of the Catholic Church in the two centuries before. Immobilists thwarted renewal and reform after the 1789 French Revolution, rejected the Enlightenment, and challenged the political liberalism of the nineteenth century. The Church was irreformable because it was impeccable, immobilists believed.

This mentality emerged full-blown in the reign of Pope Pius IX (1846–1878) and continued right up to the dawn of the Second Vatican Council.

The Church as a "beleaguered fortress" reached its decisive form in the eighteenth century with the rise of statism: the political conviction that civil rulers should control the institutional affairs of the Church in their territories, leaving the pope only a spiritual hegemony.

Here was an evolution of the "cuius regio, eius religio" (basically, the ruler's religion rules his realm) principle of the Reformation era, and the struggles over control of Church affairs in the sixteenth and seventeenth centuries. The popes naturally opposed this, but they did so ineffectively. Moreover, they themselves were civil rulers of the papal states, a considerable territory that ran across the center of the Italian peninsula, from the Mediterranean to the Adriatic Sea.

This struggle culminated in 1773 when Pope Clement XIV was pressured to suppress the Society of Jesus. France, Spain and Portugal had already expelled the Jesuits and were finally able to make the pope disband the Society altogether. Interestingly, the Society survived in Prussia and Russia, because those rulers declined to publish the pope's edict suppressing it.

Pope Clement unwittingly undermined his own authority by disbanding the Jesuits, losing a powerful intellectual advocate who would oppose civil rulers who more and more meddled in Church affairs. This was the first massive assault against the authority of the pope in modern times; it in effect undermined the concept of a global Catholic community that transcended local and national interests.

French revolutionaries made the next major assault. The French assembly created a state constitutional church in 1790, and expelled thousands of clergy who would not swear allegiance to it. The pope condemned the civil constitution but was powerless to do anything about it. With the imprisonments that followed, mediocre Catholics were swept into the revolutionary fervor, and resistant Catholics who survived underground became so intransigent that they became known as "right wing French Catholics."

Ironically these times presented a certain Christian unity, because Napoleonic rules eventually restricted Catholic and Protestant activities.

When Napoleon in 1799 seized the reins of power

in the shambles of the revolution, he was prepared to restore Catholic Christianity as the religion of France but under his control. Napoleon overthrew the papal government and brought Pope Pius VI (1775-1799) to France. Meanwhile French soldiers looted Rome of its many treasures. With the defeat of Napoleon in 1814-15, the French had to return most of those treasures.

The next pope, Pius VII (1800-1823), made some accommodations with Napoleon, thanks to a capable secretary of state: Cardinal Ercole Consalvi. A concordat, barely accepted by Rome, was then scuttled by a unilateral action of Napoleon (the so-called Organic Articles of 1802) which subordinated the Church to Napoleon; he would nominate bishops and the pope would confirm.

The situation worsened when Napoleon had the House of Savoy (Piedmont) take over papal state territories in northeastern central Italy. Napoleon went on to tell Consalvi that he would destroy the Church. Consalvi reportedly replied to Napoleon, "If in 1,800 years we clergy have failed to destroy the Church, do you really think that you'll be able to do it?" Some consider Consalvi's memorable statement appropriate in light of the clergy sexual abuse crisis in the Church today.

Pius VII finally excommunicated Napoleon for sending his army into the papal states, and Napoleon responded by abducting Pius VII to France.

After Napoleon was overthrown, Pius VII wanted to be independent of civil rulers. Liberalism was identified with hostility toward Christianity in general and Catholic Christianity in particular. Consequently, resistant or anti-revolutionary Catholics in France became anti-liberal.

In the aftermath of the French Revolution, the Church appeared at the Congress of Vienna opposed to everything that sounded like "liberte, egalite, fraternite."

Popes Leo XII (1823-1829) and Gregory XVI (1831-46) reinforced the Church's anti-democratic, anti-liberal stance. For example, a Catholic movement began to seek a rapprochement with ideas of the emerging "modern world." French Catholic priests Hugues-Felicite and Robert de Lamennais wanted the Church to assimilate democratic principles, stand against tyrannies and champion the rights of people, not rulers. Pope Gregory XVI condemned these ideas in his encyclicals *Mirari Vos* and *Singulari Nos*. As complicated as these events were, they identified the Church as promoting monarchies at the expense of democratic institutions. Meanwhile, Gregory XVI faced revolutionary foment in his papal states.

Pope Pius IX (1846-1878) tried to tamp down foment with moderate reforms. Moderate reforms satisfy no one. Moderates who start revolutions generally lose control, radicals seize control, and revolutions quickly spin out of control. This is what happened with "Pio Nono." When he tried to institute timely reforms – too rapidly for reactionaries and not fast enough for revolutionaries – the latter became more agitated.

The "risorgimento heroes" Giuseppe Mazzini, Camillo di Cavour and Giuseppe Garibaldi called for a united Italy. Pius IX refused to support a war between Italian freedom fighters and Austrian occupiers. He didn't think the papal army could challenge the Austrian army. Moreover, he did not want to jeopardize the papacy's good relationship with

Austria. And as a matter of principle, he did not want to participate in a political revolution.

"Pio Nono's" refusal to take a stance cost him dearly. His popularity plummeted. The lay governor of the papal states was assassinated, and anarchy broke out in Rome. The pope escaped south to Gaeta. Rome came under populist rule. Napoleon III sent in French troops to oust the populists from Rome. Pius IX returned in 1850 to the papal states in shambles and with a French army as his protector. Austria wanted northeast Italy, the freedom fighters wanted one country, and the French wanted to protect the pope and yet also to befriend the freedom fighters. After all, "liberte, egalite, fraternite" was still the clarion call.

Meantime Pius IX was determined to reassert his primacy over the papal states. This brought him into conflict with the risorgimento secularists who wanted one Italy. That movement overnight became anti-clerical and anti-Church. Indeed, the modern world, as the pope and his unenlightened advisers saw it, was an enemy of the clergy and hence an enemy of the Church.

The "Church against the modern world" mindset was the frame of reference for the ensuing statements of Pius IX. This "siege mentality" continued right up to the Second Vatican Council.

Pius IX challenged the Piedmontese legislation that secularized monasteries and schools and marriage laws in his 1861 proclamation *Jamdudum Cernimus*. He went further in 1864 with *Quanta Cura*, denouncing the modern spirit in general. Then came the *Syllabus of Errors* in which eighty propositions were announced and anathematized as erroneous, one of them being "that the

Pope had to reconcile himself to the idea of the modern world and of progress."

The pope realized he had to show that he had the support of the entire Church. The first Vatican Council, in 1869-70, promulgated a Constitution on the Church and a dogma on the pope's infallibility, stating by papal intervention that the pronouncements of the pope "ex cathedra" are infallible and irreformable (sans reference to episcopal consensus). This papal claim prompted a new Church schism (that is, the Old Catholic movement): another hurdle to unity.

As the Vatican approved papal infallibility in the dogmatic constitution *Pastor Aeternus*, Napoleon III declared war on Prussia. The French garrison withdrew from Rome, leaving the pope with only Swiss ceremonial guards. Prussia defeated France at Sedan in France, and the Piedmontese general Cardona came to the gates of Rome. The Swiss guards surrendered after a token battle, the pope fled behind the Vatican walls, and Italy annexed the papal states. From 1870 until 1929, popes became prisoners at the Vatican.

Then the Lateran Treaties (later confirmed in the Italian Constitution) recognized Vatican City as an independent state, with the Italian government agreeing to give the Church financial compensation for the loss of papal states.

A new emphasis was emerging in Church documents. Leo XIII and Pius XI issued major social justice encyclicals, *Rerum Novarum* (1891) and *Quadragesimo Anno* (1931). But by and large, the Roman curia maintained the status quo: the Church would continue "semper idem" – "always the same."

In the first half of the twentieth century the spirit of Pius IX — a fortress mentality and a resistance to change and adaptation—generally dominated the Roman curia.

No wonder, then, when Pope John XXIII announced a Council, and embraced the motto "Ecclesia semper reformanda" – "The Church is always reformable" (a phrase popularized by Swiss Reformed theologian Karl Barth), the news was greeted with surprised silence. The curia would certainly ensure the status quo.

The first official response to the Council call was a commission letter to all the bishops, and later to faculties of theology and canon law in Catholic universities and seminaries, requesting suggested topics and issues. The resulting 9,520 pages of material were reduced to preliminary proposals for discussion.

Meanwhile, Pope John had constituted ten preparatory commissions plus three secretariats to draft the initial schemata to be submitted to the bishops. Pope John was very interested in the work of these commissions. When the Council met, Pope John assumed, the sessions would be brief, and the bishops would approve them. This would have been the Ecumenical Council that would have "renovated and reformed the Church" without substantial change.

The vision and the agenda were not quite in sync. The Council was to hold fast to immutable truth, perfectly and perennially possessed by the Roman Catholic Church. It was to maintain the hierarchical structures and promote unity by returning to the Church. At the same time, it was to bring the Church into dialogue with the modern mindset.

Aggiornamento in discipline and polity, immobilism in doctrine and piety. How to reconcile this tension?

Cardinal Bea and his Secretariat for Promoting Christian Unity garnered the progressive notions on Christian unity, ecclesiology, religious liberty, Christian and non-Christian relations which were scattered through the fifteen volumes of episcopal proposals and largely ignored by the Theological Commission, which had primary oversight over the agenda and was chaired by Cardinal Alfredo Ottaviani. One way and another, Bea's Secretariat became the most influential single agency for the progressive cause in the new Council, effective out of all proportion to its size and original charter.

Bea had been instrumental in the preparation of Pope Pius XII's encyclical *Divino Afflante Spiritu*: a watershed in Catholic biblical circles because it allowed, in a limited fashion, for critical use of modern historical methodology in the study of Scripture. Bea was also a confidant of the pope and had gathered around him a small cadre of ecumenists: Fr. Johannes Willebrands, Fr. Frans Thyssen, Bishop Pierre Duprey, and Fr. Thomas Stransky.

On the eve of the Council only a minority of the Council bishops grasped the issues that lay before them. Within this minority, 200-300 were conservative and in control, and another 200 were uncommitted in one way or another, but more inclined to go along with the curia management than to protest.

How they came down on the progressive side of all but a few issues before the Council is the story of Vatican II. It was unpredictable.

The Council began with a crisis. A list of names for

the commissions was introduced with the expectation that they would be accepted as submitted. The bishops would not be a rubber stamp. A frail, elderly cardinal—Achille Lienart of Lille, France—stood and said the Council should adjourn immediately to caucus the bishops. Another elderly cardinal—Josef Frings of Cologne, Germany—said he agreed.

Suddenly, it was a new ball game. Actually, it was the making of the Council. Fall, 1962 was a time of tensions and nothing official was accomplished. Session Two began in Fall 1963 with a new pope and a new situation. To many Protestant observers, the so-called immobilists — curia management — were on the defensive.

Paul VI was the first Catholic leader in
four centuries to visit Geneva

Pope Paul VI meant to move the Church forward as far and as fast as possible, without risking schism. Paul's leadership, listening to the diehards as well as the reformers, is perhaps one of the most underestimated performances in the Council. The main achievement was that more than 2,000 bishops were re-educated in the give-and-take of debate. And after a useless attempt at secrecy in Session One, the main proceedings were made public, so people could follow the process. Note the Council process:

Preparatory schemata were debated, then referred back to the commissions with written amendments or interpretations. Then new drafts were prepared and submitted to the bishops for a vote: "yes" or "no" or "yes with amendments." Thus, the commissions were beholden to the bishops, and the bishops were dependent on the commissions. There was a slow, deliberate shift among the majority of bishops.

The *Dogmatic Constitution on the Church* in 1964 highlighted a basic theological insight of the Church as "the people of God" and recognized non-Roman congregations as ecclesial communities. The Roman Catholic Church made a dramatic entrance into the ecumenical movement in the constitution's second chapter:

"The Church recognizes that in many ways she is linked with those who, being baptized, are honored with the name of Christian...For there are many who honor sacred Scripture...They believe in God the Father Almighty and in Christ...They are consecrated by baptism through which they are united with Christ. They also recognize and receive other sacraments within their own churches or ecclesial communities...We can say that in some real way they are joined with us in the spirit, for to them also He gives His gifts and graces and is thereby operating among them with His sanctifying power."

The 1964 *Decree on Ecumenism* specifies in its third

chapter facets of Christian thinking and living that characterize "these separated churches and ecclesial communities" in the West:

- confession of Christ as sole mediator between God and man
- deep love and expert studies of Scripture
- baptism as incorporation into Christ
- the Eucharist as commemoration of the Lord's death and resurrection
- a lively sense of justice and a true neighborly charity
- a morality that looks to Christ and the gospel as the source of virtue.

The phrase "their own churches or ecclesial communities" would be commonplace from a Protestant frame of reference. But from a Roman Catholic reference, this was a coup de grace to a stance that had consistently characterized Catholic thinking.

The Catholic thesis had long argued that the grace of God is undeniably operative outside the visible structure of Roman Catholicism. There are Protestants with total commitment to Christ, with love for God's word and God's children, in their quest for peace and justice, in their willingness to die for the gospel. God's grace is there; but (so the thesis went) as individuals, not because they are *members* of the Lutheran or Presbyterian or Methodist *churches*.

Grace-filled individuals? Of course. Any other conclusion would defy experience. But grace-filled communities? Such pluralism (so the longtime thesis stood) would seem to contradict the divine design for salvation, the one community to which Christ has committed his saving word and his saving sacraments.

That once widespread attitude about communities is incompatible with the *Dogmatic Constitution on the Church* and the *Decree on Ecumenism*. The grace of Christ is at work, *richly and incessantly*, not only within individual Protestants but within Protestantism, within Anglicanism, etc.

This nuanced attitude has far-reaching theological implications.

It is the basis for dialogue not merely between individuals but primarily between the churches—dialogue that can deal with the other on an equal footing.

It is the profound basis for tomorrow's theology: an authentic theology where separated Christians are not adversaries of particular doctrines, but brothers and sisters in a *common concern*.

In recognizing Protestant churches as grace-filled communities, we disregard non-Roman theology only at the risk of impoverishing our own community. We must take seriously not simply their prophets' remarkable insights—Tillich and Niebuhr, Bonhoeffer and Marilyn McCord Adams (just as many Protestants revere Catholics such as Mother Teresa). We must also take seriously their Christian *communities* because these are communities of grace and salvation.

Hence, it will not do to say, "Some of my best friends are Protestants."

We must go out to the other communities in their *communal aspects.* For the community which is Methodist,

Presbyterian, etc. is alive with the presence of Christ, is a grace-filled community where the redemptive purposes of a God who wants *all people* to be saved are being worked out through the outpouring of the Holy Spirit.

This indeed was a significant development, setting Catholicism within the ongoing movement toward Christian unity. Imagine some visionary in the early twentieth century prophesying what came to be called the ecumenical revolution of the 1960s. Certainly it would have been called preposterous. And yet there we were mid-century, at the beginning of an ecumenical venture which opened up frontiers which we are still trying to settle, moving from diatribe to dialogue.

When I began my doctoral studies in 1968, in this new emerging era, I found myself pursuing the search for the authentic Christian tradition among mainstream Protestant churches. I focused my dissertation on the ways the Theological Commission on Tradition and Traditions, the Commission on Faith and Order, and the World Council of Churches, examined the question of the one Tradition and the many traditions.

The starting point was the Third World Conference on Faith and Order, held in Lund, Sweden in 1952; the endpoint, the Fourth World Conference on Faith and Order, held in Montreal, Canada in 1963. It was an attempt, primarily by groups of theologians, to grapple with Christ's hope "that they all may be one."

A Case Study In
Theological Dialogue

Consensus in doctrine and polity was regarded as a prime goal of ecumenical discussions at the start of the Faith and Order movement. Though some doubted that an undisputable formulation was possible or desirable, others reasoned that if Christians could explain themselves to each other, they would remove misconceptions and reveal areas of agreement.

In 1952, at the third World Conference on Faith and Order at Lund, Sweden, discussions focused on the separate histories of the divided churches, and the complexity in understanding any other tradition besides one's own.

According to the Conference paper, tradition "involves a certain forming of the Christian mind, often in its subconscious depths...Non-theological factors of many sorts (historical, racial, national, and so forth), many elements of group psychology, interact with theological factors in forming a tradition over the course of years."

Every effort must seek out the spirit behind the letter of a tradition or dogma, and must discern how it tried to preserve an identity and continuity with the normative apostolic tradition.

Moreover, each tradition has its own denominational hermeneutics or interpretations. Christians interpret Scripture in their Lutheran ways, their Anglican ways, etc. The appeal to Scripture, therefore, did not overcome the impasse.

The problem was not solved by comparative theology, which presupposed that each tradition was a "closed" system. "At its best," the Conference paper noted, "comparative ecclesiology could scarcely do more than clarify the actual issues in disagreement. At its worst, it allowed for self-justification in moods that varied from smug intransigence to pious truculence."

The Lund delegates realized the time was ripe for a new study.

Identity

The crucial challenge in every age is identity and continuity. "The apostolic tradition must be traditioned, and not simply repeated; else it becomes lifeless. The traditions must be criticized and reformed, and not simply maintained; else they become archaic or even decadent. But this demands that the Christian community assume the responsibility of correlating its multiple forms of interpretation with its essential form of revelation."

The problem of Tradition and traditions raised still deeper questions about the ways in which the traditionary process operated in the separate histories of the divided churches, in crisis situations, where traditions were in transit from one nation to another, one culture to another, one age to another.

"We need a historically honest answer to the question 'How has the Gospel been received, expressed and transmitted in the succeeding generations of the people of God?'" Albert Outler observed. "We need to study in an ecumenical perspective the crucial fissions which have occurred in the course of Christian history, not now to justify them, but to find a way beyond them and their divisive influence on us."

The Conference established a Theological Study Commission "to explore more deeply the resources for further ecumenical discussion to be found in that common history which we have as Christians and which we have discovered to be longer, larger and richer than any of our separate histories in our divided churches." This resolution was variously interpreted. Yet Lund had stumbled onto a way beyond the impasse.

Is there, asked Georges Florovsky, an Orthodox priest, a describable common tradition in all existing communities which call and profess themselves Christian? He underscored that the many interpretative traditions are not indefinitely plural and not arbitrarily different. The different traditions, each of which professed to be a faithful interpretation of Scripture and an authentic expression of apostolic Christianity, had to understand themselves – and the other traditions – primarily in the light of their common history.

Contemporary theologians had to enter a common investigation and be willing to admit that the Holy Spirit was at work in the other churches: and may have led to important insights into the totality of Christian life.

The most important part of the Christian heritage, common to all churches, was Scripture. It formed a constitutive element in gauging the authenticity of the many interpretative traditions which had evolved. The great question, however, was how the many interpretations of the Christ-Event were to be understood. The churches did not arrive at the same conclusions because their denominational hermeneutics were not the same.

The tragedy for Christianity was that these traditions became divisive and exclusive in the course of time. Lutheran theologian Kristen Skydsgaard stressed the fact that all the churches were trying to get deeper insight into the one faith: "They all acknowledge the authority of Holy Scripture and appeal to the true transmission of the biblical, apostolic witness. But they differ in the understanding both of the content of this witness and of the way of its transmission."

A study of tradition in a biblical and historical perspective was timely and urgent. Still some questioned whether the word "tradition" was the right entry word.

The Theological Commission on Tradition and Traditions studied and groped toward "that common history which we have as Christians and which we have discovered to be longer, larger and richer than any of our separate histories."

The North American theologians primarily observed specific cases of "traditions in transit" — in the ante-Nicene Church, the Reformation, and modern North American Christianity — and the extent to which historiography can give a true account of the history which is common to all Christians. They met three times within three years; all had commitments which precluded full-time work on the project. They groped for the answer to the question "What do our plural traditions have in common that warrants our calling them Christian in some sense?"

For ten years, the European theologians systematically examined the relationship between Scripture, Tradition and the Church from a biblical, dogmatic, and historical point of view. They regrettably did not have in their group the two people who took the initiative in the whole work: Outler and Florovsky.

In all Christian traditions there lived *the* Tradition: the self-disclosure of God to people in the saving acts of Jesus Christ, which were handed down from generation to generation. The different traditions were different interpretations of this self-disclosure of God to people, uniquely chiseled in Scripture by Christians more than nineteen centuries ago.

One way and another, the theologians debated pre-reflectively and reflectively the problem of the identity and continuity of the Gospel in the traditions of the churches, and the hot potato of doctrinal development.

They tried to clarify the relationship between the revelation of God and the different forms in which the saving acts of God in Jesus Christ were embodied: between the *traditum* and the transmission or *actus tradendi*. There never existed a "pure" word of God, separated from a human response. Nevertheless, they must be distinguished carefully.

Whether the churches expressed in their lifestyles

a greater or lesser fullness of *the* Tradition increasingly became the most pressing question.

Scripture is never alone

The North American theologians agreed substantially with the Reformation slogan *sola scriptura* "insofar as it asserts and identifies *the* Tradition as the prime datum of the Christian Testament." However, they equally concurred that *sola scriptura* was an inadequate catchword without qualification, or when it rejected the evidence for the living Tradition throughout the ages. That *Scriptura numquam sola* — Scripture was never alone — was a historical fact. Tradition was primordial.

Secondly, they agreed that *the* Tradition in the Jewish Testament was manifested in a plurality of traditions.

Thirdly, the North American group admitted that in the transplanting of Christianity from one region to another, one culture to another, and in the resulting indigenization there always existed the possibility of corrupting as well as enriching the Tradition.

But their report had some notable omissions.

First, tradition (lower case singular) "includes both the process of transmission from person to person, region to region, generation to generation, and also the substantive contents of what is transmitted." This overlooked the sacraments, which unite a recollection of Christ's Passover, the present event of grace, and the eschatological kingdom of God. Moreover, the kingdom of God was not only future but *present*. Tradition extended to all times and to all places the same Christ.

The second key category was traditions (lower case plural): the particular, historical forms by which *the* Tradition came to women and men.

The criterion was Scripture. But was not the Church also a criterion? Moreover, were there not in the Roman Catholic Church many traditions and many theologies within *the* Tradition? The Catholic position argued that the magisterium was a gift of grace, not an absolute judge. The magisterium had the assistance of the Holy Spirit in the preservation and renewal of the depositum fidei, which was locatable in Scripture and the tradition of the Church.

Sermon on the Mount

Transmitting Jesus Christ

The third key category was *the* Tradition. The content of *the* Tradition was Jesus Christ: "*The* Tradition is the self-givenness of God in the self-giving of Jesus Christ 'for us men and for our salvation' (Nicene Creed)."

The doctrinal and moral teachings of Jesus Christ also belonged to *the* content of the Tradition.

The report overemphasized Christ delivered and did not emphasize enough Christ transmitted. Also, did not the person of Christ include the whole Christian mystery, especially the sacraments, and the essential institutions of the renewed people of God?

The Christian mystery comprised the life of the Church. In the experience of this life the Church understood better the realities as well as the texts which spoke about them. Hence the lived experience of the Church in every age, for example, the writings of the desert Fathers and the saints and the theologians, the liturgical texts, the magisterial teachings, Christian art, and the practices of the people were sources of development in the Church's own self-understanding.

Moreover, the Church through its preaching and liturgy transmitted the Christian mystery to other times and places.

Finally, the report led some to believe that the Church was not really the recipient of *the* Tradition. But did not Catholic theology attribute *the* Tradition first to the Church in which the indwelling Spirit guaranteed unity, continuity, and life in the truth? The Church was the created and historical subject of *the* Tradition; the Spirit, the transcendent subject beyond history.

In sum, the North American theologians did not adequately specify the meaning of the phrase "our common history as Christians." Nor could they agree upon criteria whereby they might identify *the* Tradition.

They recognized that the exercise highlighted "the

crisis of death and transfiguration which stands between our present state of division and the full reality of the unity we seek."

Ecumenical historiography would oblige the churches to acknowledge change and thus to formulate an adequate theory of change. In this way the movement might progress toward a future in which Christians would share more fully, in some visible measure, their common life in the Body of Christ.

They acknowledged that no one church could be so completely confident of its own ability to interpret the activity of the Spirit in a tradition that it could assert categorically that it had nothing to learn from the working of the Spirit in other traditions.

Among the European theologians, Skydsgaard noted that Biblical research has shown that the oral proclamation of the Gospel preceded the written Gospel.

Moreover, "the apostolic preaching, the formulations of the creed, and the Holy Scripture itself consisted of human words, inspired by the Holy Spirit, but nevertheless human. The act of God and the human answer to it in faith belong together. Human experience has its place also in the earliest apostolic tradition… Unity in the Church was not a theological, doctrinal uniformity, but unity in faith… Man is never a 'tabula rasa,' nor is the Gospel a ready-made once for all worded manifesto, but a proclamation in a form proper to the actual condition in which [people] are living, shaped to some extent by the particular situation in time and space. Because Christ is the living Lord, the Gospel incarnates itself in different forms. The saving message is always the same, because Christ is always the same, but the expression and the interpretation turn out to be different in different contexts."

Modern historiography also forced the Protestant churches to reconsider the problem of tradition. Christianity was not indefinitely plural, Skydsgaard emphasized. The substance of tradition was Jesus Christ. Different elements of tradition served as vehicles for Christ.

Thus, the report rejected enthusiasm which disregarded human forms and words, and also rejected traditionalism which regarded *only* human forms and words. The Spirit who dwells in the midst of the Church enables men and women to chart a middle course between a sort of Homer's Scylla and Charybdis.

Skydsgaard summed up by submitting three fields which had to be explored in the dialogue regarding Scripture and tradition.

First, Scripture could not be separated from the Church. Only in the Church was Scripture rightly understood. He saw the importance of John Henry Newman's principle that the "earlier" was interpreted in the light of the "later." At the same time, the original had to illuminate critically everything that came later.

Secondly, Scripture was primary evidence of God's acts and words to man. Historically, the Bible was later than the Church, to which it owed its existence. Theologically, as a witness to the great acts of God and his word to his people, it was "before" and "above" the Church.

Thirdly, Skydsgaard urged theologians not to identify the Word of God as the doctrine of the Church. Doctrine always had to be a servant of the Word of God. It was not the Word of God itself. This raised the question of the substance of doctrine and the forms in which the substance could be expressed.

Finally, Skydsgaard gave an eschatological dimension to Scripture. Scripture pointed to the future. The kingdom of God was present but not fully present. The Church was a people on pilgrimage.

Jean-Louis Leuba drew up areas in which agreement seemed possible. Protestants recognized that tradition was an essential element of Christianity, and the European theologians agreed that the Holy Spirit actualized here and now the "then and there" presence of Christ. They also believed "a distinction must be drawn between *the* Tradition (reality as it is in Christ, handed down through history since his incarnation) and the traditions (more or less temporary expressions of that Tradition)." Scripture and the Church were inseparable in the search for a criterion.

Leuba did bring to light that the Roman Catholic and Orthodox positions maintained that the Church decided where the authentic Tradition was to be found, whereas the Protestant position maintained that Scripture decided where the Church existed and thus where authentic tradition was to be found. He underscored that the Catholic position did not mean that all traditions automatically became part of *the* Tradition, and the Protestants recognized that Church history contained actualizations of the witness of the apostles as found in Scripture. Both sides realized Church and Scripture must complement one another.

Also, the Protestant and Orthodox positions insisted that the faith was the same throughout history. The

Letter to the Hebrews expressed: "Jesus Christ is the same yesterday, today, and forever" (Hebrews 13:8). In a sense, the history of the Church has been a receiving and a living out of all the Christian values summed up in the human consciousness of the Risen Christ.

Catholic theology underscores the presence of the Spirit in the Church who enables Christians in every age to grasp the indefinite implications of the self-disclosure of God to humans in Jesus Christ. The magisterium through the assistance of the Holy Spirit both teaches and is itself taught. The last word belongs to the Holy Spirit and to his human instrument, set up by God among his people.

The relationship between the Risen Christ and his Church is covenantal, not hypostatic. The Church has moments of grace and sin, faithfulness and unfaithfulness. Humans are free and responsible. The ultimate gauge of the Church's faithfulness to its covenant in the Catholic self-understanding is first the reality of Christ summed up in the totality of tradition. It communicates much more than can be expressed in human language. In the liturgy the totality of tradition is uniquely preserved and communicated.

The Reformers shortchanged the activity of the Spirit, whose work they limited primarily to the individual understanding of Scripture.

Yves Congar observed that "The difference between the Reformation Churches and us could well be one of ecclesiology rather than of hermeneutics here. Once again it seems to me that Protestant thought separates Christ in too radical a manner from his Body, the Church. Failing to recognize sufficiently that by the sending of Christ and his Spirit God has truly entered into history, it isolates in an excessive manner the ephapax (once for all) of Christ from its effects in humanity, which effects it plays down in order to exalt the sovereignty of the Lord. It misconstrues the significance of the Mass...and ignores the value of the Tradition."

Today, most scholars recognize that Scripture was never the only means by which the Church received the apostolic faith. However, Scripture is an indispensable reference. Jesus Christ, who put nothing in writing, gave to men and women in every age the gift of himself through the Church, the Spirit, and the apostolic ministry.

Scripture, Tradition, and the Church (us) together continually interact in the "explicitation" of that self-disclosure.

A summary

European theologians met in August 1962 in Copenhagen, Denmark for the seventh and final time. A volume of essays was published in German, as *Schrift und Tradition*, edited by Skydsgaard and Vischer.

Skydsgaard's essay on "Tradition and the Word of God — A Contribution to the Ecumenical Dialogue" focused on the perception of revelation. Except for the question of justification, no other question had been so offensive to Roman Catholic theology.

Into the Middle Ages the canonical writings and their interpretation in the Church were viewed as a unity, Skydsgaard observed. "The Fathers, and theologians such as Bonaventure and Thomas Aquinas considered Scripture as the sole basis for the faith," he declared, "but it must be remembered that sacra scriptura included the theology of the Fathers as the correct interpretation of the Scripture."

Moreover, the term sacra scriptura was used more and more for the books of the Bible: "Over against it stood the Church with her authority, the gathered hierarchy with the Pope at its head."

In this atmosphere at the beginning of the sixteenth century, Martin Luther had fired a broadside by insisting on sola scriptura. In the initial confusion, the theologians were sure of one thing: The Holy Spirit guided the Church in understanding Scripture correctly. Skydsgaard noted that "hardly any other period of Church History has made such diligent use of the words in Saint John 16: 12-13." ("I have much more to tell you, but you cannot bear it now. But when he comes, the Spirit of truth, he will guide you to all truth.")

Skydsgaard then called attention to the uncertainty at the Council of Trent. The opinions seemed almost irreconcilable. One would have to admire the moderation in the final draft of the Decree of April 8, 1546. Skydsgaard summarized the final draft of that decree:

"The revelation, the Gospel, is to be considered in terms of 'truth' and 'discipline,' that is, doctrine and rules of life. The article refers only to the apostolic traditions and to those which have to do with faith and life…These apostolic traditions which do not consist of redeeming truths but rather of general rules for worship and the administration of the sacraments, together with certain moral commandments, are to be honored in the same way as Scripture…However, one thing is certain: the Lutheran principle of sola scriptura is rejected as heretical…clearly limited to apostolic Scripture and the apostolic traditions. With the death of the last apostle it was concluded."

The Reformers' idea of the unfolding or development of doctrine was considered a sign of heresy.

Skydsgaard described the later understanding: "The weight was shifted more and more to the present authority of the Church…The guidance of the Holy Spirit is no longer seen only in the faithful preservation and the correct understanding by the Church of the apostolic faith as given in the apostolic writings and in the apostolic traditions, but rather more—and latterly—in the present authority of the Church when she speaks and acts."

The emphasis, then, shifted from the original Gospel to the authority of the Church. Skydsgaard added that since the nineteenth century "the trend has been to interpret tradition as traditio viva, as the living interpretation of Sacred Scripture…Its true element is the Church as a living organism permeated with the Holy Spirit."

Two representatives of this view were Mohler and Newman.

Johann Mohler took the Church as "the essential form of Christianity, indeed the Church is at all times the continuation of the humanity of Christ…In Jesus of Nazareth the eternal Word, the Son, takes on human nature. In the Church the continued eternal revelation of Christ takes place; here Christ is present. Christ takes on the human form of the Church."

In light of this, Skydsgaard found Mohler defined tradition subjectively ("the peculiar Christian sense present in the Church and propagating itself through

Christian education...the enduring Word living in the hearts of the faithful.") and objectively ("the total faith of the Church found in the external historical witnesses throughout all centuries.")

The living Word in the heart, the Word which became faith, was what lived, expanded, and matured in the tradition of the Church. This was the sensus fidelium or sensus christianus populi fidelis, which, led by the hierarchical principle of the Church, is at all times in agreement with the original faith, even if the form and expression differ.

Skydsgaard then showed how Mohler connected Scripture and tradition. "The concept of scripture as a revealed communication, as God's word, is connected with the concept of the Divine word which becomes human faith. The Word of Scripture becomes identical with the Word living in the Church...If faith rests only on Scripture as an isolated book, isolated from tradition, we have built on sand and one day the Church will certainly collapse."

Simultaneously, though independently of Mohler, John Henry Newman dealt with Scripture and tradition.

The Protestant principle of sola scriptura, Newman protested, ultimately ended up in skepticism: "Sacred Scripture was not written to instruct about doctrine as a whole, but rather to illuminate those who had already been instructed in it (see Newman, Via Media, I, 58). The Church, as a living historical reality, with its creed, and its doctrine, its discipline and its order, existed before [the Bible]. All these things existed at first in embryo; but they were there before [the Bible]. Therefore, those who wish to base their creed solely on the Bible must undeniably fall away from the Church."

In Newman's Essay on the Development of Christian Doctrine written immediately before his conversion in 1845, he realized that none of the churches truly reflected the Early Church. "With regard to the Roman Church," he wrote, "the main difference appears to be that it teaches much more than the Early Church," a fact which earlier formed Newman's main argument against the Roman Church.

Skydsgaard notes that "The richer the idea is, the more abundant and nuanced is our understanding of this idea, and the more will it, in the course of time, realize its various aspects in perception. Now, Newman compares Christianity with such a pregnant idea. An 'idea' has been given to the Church, God's revelation is Jesus Christ."

In other words, from the beginning everything is given in the "divine illic et tunc" *as a beginning.* The succeeding ages are "developments, arising out of a keen and vivid realizing of the Divine Depositum of Faith." (see Newman's *Apologia Pro Vita Sua*, 209)

Skydsgaard called attention to the fact that for Newman, "the Event of Jesus Christ, as God's direct Word, is something unique and special, but that it has been carried forward organically into the continued age of the Church, that is, into tradition. The incarnation in Christ is continued in tradition. The presence of Christ becomes the existence of the Church in continued time."

Skydsgaard then evaluated the understanding of tradition. Everyone lived in tradition. Moreover, cultural, historical, psychological, and sociological factors all played a part in the history of Christianity. The history of Christianity is a constant testimony to Tradition and traditions which are indissolubly interwoven to the passing on of the various formulations of the faith, to definite expressions of human piety and worship.

Luther did not oppose Scripture to tradition as such, but rather laid the basis for a new understanding of tradition. Luther tried to strip away the non-essentials and concentrate on the essential, that is, Jesus Christ, his words and deeds, his life and death, his rising from the dead.

Roman Catholic theology argued that Scripture was interpreted correctly in the Church, and in the sense which the Church had always given it. The prime Catholic hermeneutical principle, Skydsgaard declared, was: "That which comes earlier is understood and interpreted by means of that which comes later." In other words, Scripture became intelligible in the light of later development. The words of institution at the Lord's Supper are understood on the basis of the Church's doctrine of the Lord's Supper; the scattered statements about Mary are understood on the basis of Mariology, and so forth.

Skydsgaard admitted a truth in this principle. Roman Catholic theology assumed that which came "later" was the unfolding of the revelation of Jesus Christ under the guidance of the Holy Spirit. Roman Catholic hermeneutics was "a hermeneutics of faith. There must be an understanding of this on the part of Protestants..."

One thing stood firm in Skydsgaard's opinion: "much more important than to underline the truth of the 'retrogressive' interpretation is to see that the original retains its independent power and validity. This 'original' must critically illumine everything that comes later, the whole historical reality of the Church and its tradition."

Yves Congar suggested in 1963 three categories at the root of the differences between Roman Catholics and Protestants:

1. We must tackle the question of the Church itself... The Catholic position is unintelligible apart from a certain idea of the "Body of Christ": a sacramental idea, one could say, of the Church, which is the effectual sign of the saving work of God who binds himself to the Church of the New and everlasting Covenant and indwells it. Protestant thought, on the other hand, often leaves the impression of wishing to construct the idea of Tradition while dispensing with the Church.

2. It seems that one could distinguish classical Catholic theology on the one hand, as it flows from the scholastic tradition, and the thought of the Continental Reformation on the other hand, by a concern for *realities*, that is for things, and a concern for *acts*, respectively... It is rather a question of balance. Current Catholic theology ought to be more concerned with the act of God. Protestant thought ought to affirm more clearly that the act of God reveals Jesus Christ *to the Church* and to the faithful *in the Church*.

3. It could be asked whether, finally, the difference does not come down to the idea of Revelation. Catholic theology insists on Revelation as

communication of understanding through a "locutio formalis," a Word properly so called. It has a historical and objective idea of Revelation. The Council of Trent itself, when considering tradition, speaks of "the Gospel" as something contemporary and active, less historical and objective (but this last adjective misrepresents our meaning).

Ecumenical theology must address itself seriously to the questions of ecclesiology and pneumatology and acknowledge more explicitly the experience of the mystery of Christ as the source of the magisterial teachings of the Church.

At the same time, the magisterium can only witness to the revelation of God; it does not create revelation.

The fundamental issue in the dialogue between contemporary Roman Catholic and Reformed theology may be seen as a question of the fullness of truth. What role do the Church and Tradition play in the Christian life?

Congar addressed the following question to Catholic and Reformed theology in an effort to take the dialogue another step forward:

"We are all agreed not to admit a Tradition which would be totally independent of Scripture (this is the basic minimum). The problem is as follows: is there only one authority, Scripture, or is there a proper authority in Tradition, distinct (that is, not deriving the whole of its value from Scripture) but secondary in relation to the supreme authority of Scripture? A Catholic must reply in the affirmative. Such a reply is based first of all on the existence of elements other than their writings originating from the apostles…In the concrete, we do indeed see Protestant theologians quote the Fathers and the councils, even seeking to harmonize their own thought with that of Tradition…All things considered, the basic problem is ecclesiological."

Reformed theology must ask whether Scripture is the only divinely established means whereby men and women enter into a covenantal relationship with God. It seems to many that Reformed theology does not recognize sufficiently that Scripture will provide the basic principles, but a special ministry is a constitutive element of the Church.

Perhaps the question of Tradition and traditions ultimately centers on the way in which people objectify the unique and definitive self-disclosure of God to people in the person of Jesus Christ.

Though much of Christ's revelation was communicated to the apostles in concepts and ideas, there was still much of the knowing experience between Christ and the apostles that eluded precise conceptual expression. Because of their lived experience with Christ, the apostles knew more than they could say. They received pre-predicative knowledge which they could not thematize immediately in their lifetime into neat, precise reflexive concepts.

For the apostles the propositions of apostolic theology were, in a certain sense, a development of dogma not from previous propositions, but from the more primitive and unreflexive Christ-experience. What was passed on in the fullness of the apostolic succession encompassed Word, sacrament, and authority.

Expressing the mystery of God

In the past, Catholic theologians had stressed the propositional aspect of divine revelation. During the mid-twentieth century, theologians were attempting to emphasize another aspect. It is closed in the sense that people cannot add to the objective content of the apostolic revelation; and it is open in the sense that the Church can develop it more fully.

Karl Rahner, for example, noted that doctrinal explication in its most profound dimension was a movement from pre-reflexive possession of an entire truth to its more reflexive, though necessarily partial, appropriation in and through propositional formulation. Rahner believed the key to the solution lay in a re-evaluation of the revealed utterance. What was transmitted from apostolic times was not a package of propositions but the entirety of the Christ-experience climaxing the history of salvation. The revealed utterance was part of this entirety, and it was both statement and communication.

Always, the mystery of God completely transcends man's ability to adequately express it. In fact, human thought and language prove deficient even for the adequate expression of human realities.

Christianity professes a perennial unchanging truth, but at the same time this truth is capable of greater explicitation. There are various modes of expression. Christianity is not limited to any specific culture, though it is almost always found within a cultural context. Dogmas and doctrinal formations always point beyond themselves and serve as indicators of the underlying reality, the *mystery* of God. God alone is absolute.

The expression of Christian truth in principle remains open to various possibilities. Greater understanding is achieved through clarification. Man's appropriation of divine revelation is made manifest in a progressive move: from a pre-conceptual, non-propositional, non-reflexive possession of an entire truth to a more reflexive, but partial, appropriation. There is a gradual unfolding of the original content of Christian faith.

More importantly, the language of theology must have reference to the experience of Christians in community. Edward Schillebeeckx, in a 1971 lecture on the criteria of orthodoxy, emphasized that "...the linguistic symbols of a relevant theological interpretation must throw light on our ordinary everyday personal and social existence in the world, and vice versa." He underscored that "Christianity is not simply a hermeneutical undertaking."

Unless the Christian theologian acknowledges the fact of pluralism, attempts at ecumenical unity will likely run aground. Cardinal Avery Dulles, in his book *The Survival of Dogma*, contends that the failure of Christians to acknowledge a plurality of irreducibly distinct articulations of the Word of God has contributed significantly to the divisive fragmentation of Christianity. Dulles also cautions about the limits of pluralism.

To be clear, the Word of God cannot be identified fully with any single human articulation.

Rahner maintains that pluralism in the past rested mostly upon a common philosophical foundation. Today, the philosophical underpinnings of many contemporary theologies are so diverse that these theologies, though different, may not be contradictory. Rahner incapsulates this in his article "Pluralism in Theology and the Oneness of the Church's Profession of Faith":

"We are encountering basic positions…which do not spring from a shared horizon of fundamental understanding and which do not directly contradict our own theology. The disparity is not clear cut, so that we cannot tackle it directly. In such cases we cannot adopt a clear yes or no toward the other side."

This differentiates the theological quest for doctrinal agreement and the ecumenical quest for a lived unity. Must not the churches experience a lived unity before they achieve full doctrinal accord? The language must have some reference to the lived experience in community.

Because various philosophical, historical, psychological and sociological factors share a doctrinal formulation, theological pluralism, for Rahner, is not only possible but also justifiable: "On the one hand, the magisterium may be guided by representatives of a specific theology. On the other hand, it may accord equal weight to the views of widely different theologies; in this case the insurmountable pluralistic situation in the Church will be mirrored in the magisterium itself. In either case, the Church must give much more responsibility to the theologies themselves than she has in the past…If we wish to achieve credal oneness and to verify it, then we must utter this profession together, concretely celebrate the death of the Lord together, execute the sacraments together, and engage in joint activity in the world. Through these activities the oneness and sameness of our credal profession will become real, whatever pluralism may exist in theology."

In other words, if the churches first insist on full doctrinal agreement before they can unite, they will never achieve unity.

Perhaps the most viable approach for the churches would be to acknowledge genuine tensions, and then to venture out into the unknown pilgrimage toward unity, so that together they can address themselves effectively to the role of the Church in the world.

Lukas Vischer advocates a similar polity. Unity, Vischer writes, cannot be established merely on the basis of a joint review of the past or by agreed answers to questions whose answers eluded generations. The churches have to establish unity in the present by answering together the questions which confront them in the world.

Going forth together

Hans Kung in the preface to Volume 44 of *Concilium* highlights the crescendo of impatience among Christians who want to get down to action and practical arrangements. While acknowledging the importance of theological agreement, Kung contends that many theological discussions are speculative and scarcely meet the needs of the world. He summons all the Christian churches to take some practical action. For example:

1. Unconditional and mutual recognition of each other's baptism.

2. Regular interchange of preachers and theology professors so that we can become acquainted with what we have in common and on what we disagree.
3. More frequent common services of the Word.
4. Fostering common biblical study in communities and at the academic level.
5. Increased cooperation and integration in the denominational theological faculties (e.g., common libraries for seminaries, sharing and recognition of lectures and projects).
6. Exploring possibilities for establishing a common theological and ecumenical center for basic studies.
7. Ecumenical cooperation in public life (common issues, initiatives, action).

In sum, the theological methodology seeking doctrinal agreement reached the point of diminishing returns. The time had come for the churches *together* to enter into the issues which confront the world. Agreement, these theologians said, must follow involvement in the world if the ecumenical movement and indeed the Christian community is to move beyond the impasse.

The Theological Commission on Tradition and Traditions came to a formal close in 1963 with the presentation of its report to the Fourth World Conference on Faith and Order in Montreal, Canada. For almost a decade, the theologians had become increasingly aware of the complexity and ambiguity of locating the *traditio constitutiva* in the *traditiones interpretativae.*

For these and other reasons, the mid-century harvest was meager. But it was a beginning: the first real attempt to plan specific research in the receiving, renewing, and transmitting of the Gospel. And the theologians' work made good thesis material for priests-in-training.

The Theological Commission took on more significance for Roman theologians in the tides and wake of the Second Vatical Council. The Council bishops altered many traditions and at the same time emphasized that they had not altered *the* Tradition; they simply made *the* Tradition more fully manifest in their traditions. The Council promulgated a change of traditions in the Tradition.

How Christians can embody more fully *the* Tradition, and work together in the modern world, has become an urgent and timely question, so "they may all be one." Development demonstrates ipso facto that the Roman Church is not simply *the* Tradition. Catholic traditions are capable of change to express more fully and more richly the Christian tradition. Catholic men and women have a crucial role to play. What better gift can we share as we live together the 2000th anniversary of Jesus Christ's Church?

What is needed today are criteria whereby we can distinguish between what is purely relative and what is essential to remaining faithful to an authentic Christian view.

THE CHURCH ALWAYS
REFORMABLE

"If in 1800 years we clergy have failed to destroy the
Church, do you think that you'll be able to do it?"
Cardinal Ercole Consalvi to Napoleon Bonaparte,
after the latter threatened to destroy the Church

More than a half century since the Catholic Church
entered the ecumenical movement in earnest, there
is evidence that Catholics, Orthodox and Protestants in
many ways moved from diatribe to dialogue. Conversations
between and among theologians progressed significantly
on many issues: at least in theological dialogue and
documents.

The Pontifical Council for Promoting Christian Unity,
representing over 1.2 billion Catholics, has a large library
of theological conversations with the Orthodox churches
(over 200 million members), the Anglican communion
(over 80 million in the Church of England and others),
the Lutheran World Federation (over 75 million) and the
World Communion of Reformed Churches (some 100

million), to name but four. They are accessible through the Holy See website vatican.va.

Catholic and Eastern Orthodox Christianity have a common heritage based on the Nicene Creed, and generally good relationships.

However, Patriarch Bartholomew's establishment in 2019 of an independent Orthodox church in the Ukraine exacerbated tensions between the patriarchates of Constantinople and Moscow. Catholics and Eastern Orthodox are still divided about the understanding of papal primacy vis-à-vis episcopal synodality; how these are interrelated in Christianity remains an open question.

Among the ecclesial communities of the West, the question of Anglican orders continues as a fundamental theological disagreement. The Anglican ordination of women to the presbyterate and episcopate exacerbates the issue. Divine election, the Eucharist and other sacraments, ordained ministry, and authority still remain stumbling blocks in theological discussions, and in some cases may cause further divisions.

Nor can Catholics ignore "Dominus Jesus," issued by the Congregation for the Doctrine of the Faith in 2000, during the pontificate of Pope John Paul II. Pope Benedict XVI reasserted the universal primacy of the Roman Catholic Church in 2007, approving a document of the same Congregation proclaiming "Christ established here on earth only one Church," and indicating Orthodox churches were defective and other Christian denominations cannot be called true churches because they lack apostolic succession.

Orthodox and Protestants theologians did not receive

those two documents well. The quest for Christian unity seems as elusive as ever.

Cardinal Walter Kasper, President Emeritus (2001-2010) of the Pontifical Council for Promoting Christian Unity and an accomplished theologian and prolific author, summarized ecumenical conversations between Catholic and Lutheran, Reformed, Anglican and Methodist theologians over forty years in his 2009 book *Harvesting the Fruits: Basic Aspects of Christian Faith in Ecumenical Dialogue*. The book is required reading for anyone pursuing dialogues among and between the churches. Whether these theological agreements translate to the "grass roots" is another question.

Kasper attempts to answer the basics: Where are we? Where can we and where should we go forward? To what extent have we resolved core issues over which Protestant Christians separated in the sixteenth century? What unresolved questions still need to be taken up?

Chapter one examines the fundamentals of Christian faith, Jesus Christ and the Trinity. Here Kasper finds fundamental consensus: what we share in faith is much more than what divides us.

Chapter two addresses the central issue that first sparked the sixteenth century division: salvation, justification and sanctification. Kasper notes that Catholic, Lutheran and Methodist theologians have reached substantive agreement on what was once the central problem.

The Joint Declaration on Justification of the Lutheran World Federation and Catholic Church in 1999, and the World Methodist Council in 2006 and World Communion of Reformed Churches in 2017 agreed that "In faith we together hold the conviction that justification is the work of the triune God. The Father sent his Son into the world to save sinners. The foundation and presupposition of justification is the incarnation, death and resurrection of Jesus Christ. Justification means that Christ himself is our righteousness, in which we share through the Holy Spirit in accord with the will of the Father. Together we confess: By grace alone, in faith in Christ's saving work and not because of any merit on our part, we are accepted by God and receive the Holy Spirit, who renews our hearts while equipping and calling us to good works."

Chapter three of Kasper's study covers the nature and mission of the Church, sources of authority, and ministry, especially ordained ministry, episcopacy and papacy. Substantive disagreements persist relative to these Church issues.

Chapter four summarizes the sacraments, especially baptism and Eucharist. Kasper finds fundamental agreement on baptism and a convergence in the understanding of the Eucharist, though some issues of Eucharist are still unresolved.

Nevertheless, Kasper is optimistic about the future of Christian unity. He emphasizes not what divides, but what unites Christians, especially our common confession of the triune God and Jesus Christ as Savior and Lord. Through our common baptism, he writes, we have an incomplete communion between the Catholic Church and its dialogue partners. The churches have a better understanding of the relation between Scripture and *tradition*, a basic agreement on the doctrine of justification, and a clearer understanding of the nature of the Church.

Kasper concludes with important questions still to be discussed. For example, how to interpret the Bible in the light of the Church's tradition? What does it mean to be a human person in light of God's design for us? What are the sources of authority in the Church, and in particular, what is the role of the pope? And what about the vexing question of inter-communion?

Kasper acknowledges that the churches have different ideas about these issues: "there are deficits, or rather wounds stemming from division and wounds deriving from sin also in the Catholic Church. Nonetheless, there are important elements of the Church of Christ outside the visible Catholic Church."

Is the ecumenical movement in the doldrums now? Not so, for Kasper. There is much to be thankful for; and what has been achieved could not even have been dreamed of when these dialogues began. They have established common ground to progress with further dialogue and more extensive common witness to Jesus Christ in the world.

The Second Vatican Council's *Dogmatic Constitution on the Church* asserts that the Church of Christ subsists in the Catholic Church. It did not detail how "subsists in" is understood. The Council sought to harmonize two statements: the Church of Christ, despite divisions among Christians, exists only in the Catholic Church; and outside of her structure, many elements of sanctification and truth can be found. What distinguishes churches from ecclesial communities, from a Catholic viewpoint, is the sacrament of ministerial orders.

Orthodox churches do not recognize the primacy of the Petrine ministry, and therefore are defective in this light. Yes, Catholics are committed to ecumenical dialogue, but to be constructive, it must involve fidelity to identity.

"Dominus Jesus" reaffirmed that the Catholic faithful profess an historical continuity—rooted in apostolic succession—between the Church founded by Jesus Christ and the Catholic Church, and that there is a single Church of Christ, which subsists in the Catholic Church. The Orthodox churches remain united to her by means of apostolic succession and a valid Eucharist. The Church of Christ is present and operative in these churches, even though they do not accept papal primacy.

Ecclesial communities which have not preserved the valid episcopate and the substance of the Eucharistic mystery are not deemed churches in the proper sense; however, those baptized in these communities are, by baptism, incorporated into Christ and thus are in a certain communion with the Catholic Church. Hence, the Church possesses unity but lacks universality.

The mission of the Church is "to proclaim and establish the kingdom of Christ and of God, and the Church is on earth, the seed and beginning of that kingdom." Hence, there is an intimate connection between Christ, the kingdom, and the Church. The kingdom of God cannot be detached from Christ or the Church. The Church is not an end unto herself, but the seed, sign and instrument of the kingdom of God.

"Dominus Jesus" states that the Church "is necessary for salvation: the one Christ is the mediator and the way of salvation; He is present to us in the body which is the Church. Jesus Christ himself explicitly asserted the necessity of faith and baptism. Therefore, it is necessary to keep these two truths together, namely, the real possibility of salvation in Christ for all humankind and the necessity of the Church for this salvation. For those who are not formally and visibly members of the Church, salvation in Christ is accessible by virtue of a grace which, while having a mysterious relationship to the Church, does not make them formally part of the Church, but enlightens them in a way which is accommodated to their spiritual and material situation."

Hence, equality, a presupposition of inter-religious dialogue, refers to the equal personal dignity of the parties in dialogue, if not doctrinal content.

In light of the parameters established by Pope John Paul II's 2000 declaration "Dominus Jesus" and reaffirmed by Pope Benedict XVI in 2007, I would like to reemphasize a truth of good Pope John XXIII: the Church is "always reformable." When he announced in 1959 that he would convene a council for the purpose of reforming the Church, no one then could imagine the consequences, especially with regard to the search for Christian unity.

Today, the theological conversations among Catholic, Orthodox and Protestant theologians seem to have reached a point of diminishing returns. Yes, dialogue, and especially cooperation among the churches, where feasible, must continue. Cooperative social projects, wherever feasible, must be a priority, so that we may contemplate how we *walk the walk* together.

But first, the Catholic Church has work to do within itself. We need to look at ourselves periodically, at what we as Catholic servant leaders are doing. It's time to refocus on reforming the Catholic Church anew, which may become a catalyst in furthering Christian unity. Reform was a catalyst for the incredible advances in ecumenical relations among and between the churches in the 1960s and 1970s. I believe Pope John XXIII was not simplistically referring to rewriting documents. I wouldn't be surprised if he thought of Matthew 7:4-5, of getting to know ourselves, as well as one another, and "removing the wooden beam from our eye."

We can't think of looking effectively at others if we don't first look at ourselves. Cardinal Carlo Martini, the late Archbishop of Milan and a renowned scholar and popular book author, described the Catholic Church as being "200 years behind" the times. He observed: "Our culture has grown old, our churches are big and empty and the church bureaucracy rises up, our religious rites and the vestments we wear are pompous." That was in 2012.

Church attendance in Europe and the United States has dropped significantly since then, according to bishops who occasionally update their statistics. The latest Pew Research indicates 65 percent of people surveyed claim Christianity as their religion (compared to 77 percent in 2009).

On a people-in-the-pews level, unless the Church adopts a more generous attitude towards divorced persons, for example, it will lose the allegiance of future generations. The question, Martini said, is not whether divorced couples can receive holy communion, but how the Church can help complex family situations.

Martini's advice to conquer the tiredness of the Church was a "radical transformation, beginning with the pope and his bishops." The scandals of clergy sexual abuse of minors, in particular, have been a harmful logjam, undermining the credibility of priests and bishops. Martini also spoke his mind on other matters that the Vatican had in past considered taboo, including the role of women in the Church.

Martini's point was the Catholic Church needs another revolution or reformation, like the Second Vatican Council, a real look at ourselves and rigorous collaborative changes, if it is to continue to be a credible witness to the Gospel.

I, along with others, would emphasize that these changes need to be made in light of four principles:

1) the Church as the people of God (clergy, religious and laity), working collaboratively to fulfill the mission of the Church,

2) Subsidiarity at the national and local levels, wherever possible, without jeopardizing the unity of the Church,

3) more transparency in the decision-making processes of the Church, and

4) more accountability by adopting best practices in the international, national and local leadership structures of the Church.

Years ago, a colleague of mine pronounced that "transparency" and "accountability" seemed to be missing in the curia's vocabulary. A compelling point.

There are indeed various models of the Church. Cardinal Avery Dulles, for example, highlighted the

Church as institution, mystical communion, sacrament, herald and servant. Each model has its strengths and weaknesses. No model, of course, can fully capture the reality of the Church of Jesus Christ.

My preference is to emphasize the Church as the people of God. The 1964 *Dogmatic Constitution on the Church* declared that the Church is the People of God:

"...It pleased God to bring men (sic) together as one people, a people which acknowledges Him in truth and serves Him in holiness...calling together a people made up of Jew and gentile, making them one, not according to the flesh but in the Spirit. This was to be the new People of God."

The international, national and local structures of the Church should reflect more visibly the "people of God" – clergy, religious and lay men and women. Moreover, the membership of these structures should clarify whenever the membership has a deliberative or consultative voice, wherever appropriate. If membership has only a consultative voice, decision-making should include a clear, stated rationale about the method. Otherwise, the process will lack credibility. Yes, bishops in particular are entrusted with sanctifying, teaching and governing. But governance does not necessarily have to be interpreted to mean bishops are "absolute monarchs"; rather governance should be understood as servant leaders of the Gospel with transparent and accountable structures to support them as credible leaders. After all, the bishops are not immune to the effects of original sin. All of us sinners need redemption.

During a ceremony in St. Peter's Basilica, Pope Francis described the pallium, the small wool white garment placed on an archbishop, in this way: "The pallium reminds the sheep that the shepherd is called to bear him on his shoulders. It is a sign that the shepherds do not live for themselves but for the sheep."

Problems arise when bishops think they are "absolute monarchs." In the eyes of many, Theodore McCarrick, Bernard Law and Michael Bransfield could be posters for this image, appearing to use their episcopal roles – with Godly mottos like "Come Lord Jesus," "To live is Christ" and "Thy will be done" — to benefit themselves.

Like all human beings, clergy (bishops, priests and deacons) have flaws and they too require checks and balances to enjoy the reputation as credible witnesses to the Gospel. The Church is made up of saints and sinners. It's worth remembering what Cardinal Consalvi said to Napoleon: "If in 1800 years we clergy have failed to destroy the Church, do you think that you'll be able to do it?"

Many Church decisions call for a particular expertise which clergy generally are not expected to have, nor do many have. These frequently are business, legal or personnel decisions, for the common good. They require good collegial judgments. On a daily basis, laypersons—from business men and women to parents—have practical experience by necessity.

While theological conversations can and do benefit the vision of Christian unity, these conversations alone do not achieve unity. The Catholic Church must continually reform itself and be a credible and compelling witness to the Gospel.

Many ecumenical councils were convened to address and reform a Church in crisis. The cri de coeur for reform has been heard throughout the centuries: from popes like Gregory the Great (590-604AD) and Pius V (1566-1572AD) to Pope Francis, and from saintly guides such as Bernard of Clairvaux in the eleventh century, Francis and Clare of Assisi and Dominic Guzman in the thirteenth century, and Catherine of Siena in the fourteenth century. Many modern voices have called for ongoing reform, including Yves Congar, Leo Suenens, Karl Rahner, Marie-Dominique Chenu, Hans Kung, John Quinn, and Leonardo Boff, as well as several women leaders, in their own inspiring ways.

Reforms ensure that the Church is a credible witness to the Gospel and advances the prayer of Jesus "that they may all be one."

As Pope John Paul II urged in his 1995 encyclical *Ut Unum Sint*, the search for unity must *pervade the whole life of the Church*.

Ut Unum Sint calls for a discussion by *all Christians* about how best exercise the papacy. It holds up the synodal model and emphasizes that the pope is a member of the college of bishops and that primacy should be exercised collegially without compromising the primacy of the pope.

Pope Francis blesses visitors of many faiths

Pope Francis, in consultation with his Council of Cardinals, is circulating among bishops, selected academics and curia heads a draft of a new apostolic constitution tentatively titled *Praedicate Evangelium* (Preach the Gospel). It's primarily about the reform of the Roman curia, the central government of the Church and would succeed Pope John Paul II's *Pastor Bonus*.

The draft (not promulgated as of December 2019) emphasizes the Church's mission to evangelize and its charitable works, synodality, more lay people in roles of leadership and responsibility and a healthy decentralization without compromising the unity of the Church. "In accordance with the Second Vatican Council, because of this service to the Petrine ministry, the curia is also at the service of the bishops, of the episcopal conferences, of their regional and continental associations, of the particular Churches and of the other ecclesial communities," the draft states. But what precisely will be the contents of this new apostolic constitution, remains to be seen.

In sum, for true reform, the Church's structures continually must be critiqued constructively and boldly in light of its primary mission to evangelize. St. Paul, for example, made constructive criticism to St. Peter about whether Jewish practices had to be observed by gentile Christians. It was similar to the criticisms of many saints to religious authorities of their times.

Collegiality in church structures

The new constitution, to begin this new decade, hopefully will imbed more clearly and more transparently and more representatively collegiality/synodality in the structures of the Church so that there is an open exchange of ideas relative to the challenges the Church confronts. Of course, we recognize that bishops are to *sanctify*, teach and govern in real ways, yet they are not equal to the pope whose governance is decisive, even as he delegates. The pope reserves the responsibility to make final decisions or judge extraordinary cases. The pope recognizes the principle of subsidiarity—the higher authority should act only when the ordinary shows itself incapable of fulfilling its mission—but may in extraordinary circumstances intervene for the good of the universal Church.

Pope Francis, for example, convened synods to explore important topics that require a "speedy solution" and need immediate attention for the good of the entire Church. The two Synods on the Family, in 2014 and 2015, attempted to identify the current status of the family and its challenges; and then formulate pastoral guidelines to respond to these challenges. The 2016 post-synodal exhortation *Amoris Laetitia* (The Joy of Love) covered a wide range of topics related to marriage and family life as well as their contemporary challenges. It encouraged clergy especially to accompany and care for families and others in situations of particular need. However, controversy arose regarding whether Chapter 8 of the exhortation changed the Church's sacramental discipline concerning access to the sacraments of Reconciliation and the Eucharist for divorced couples who have civilly married. The Amazon synod in October 2019 discussed new paths for evangelization in the Pan-Amazon region. Particular attention was paid to indigenous people and the rain forest crisis. Pope Francis' exhortation "Querida Amazonia" – "Beloved Amazon" – complemented rather than superceded the synod's own final document. The pope's exhortation is an invitation to seek justice and solidarity. The point is that the Church has to be open to a wide exchange of ideas about evangelization, especially in synods, in order to fulfill its mission.

Laymen and laywomen in church structures

A major reform would be to include in the dicasteries and nunciatures, for example, a representative international membership of clergy, religious and laymen and laywomen. There appears to be no theological reason why a layman or laywoman can't serve as a cardinal or head a congregation or nunciature. These governing structures should have memberships that reflect their constituencies. Local governance — diocesan curias and local parishes – likewise should reflect their constituencies.

Notably, L'Osservatore Romano began this decade with a special supplement on women's roles in the Church. Conversations around the theme logically clarify that women want not simply for men to *speak* to them, about them and for them, but to *listen*.

A reform which is apparently not in the early draft would be a more detailed and more transparent process for choosing bishops of dioceses. While there are many ways of doing this world-wide, bishops generally should be chosen from the diocese in which they are incardinated: where the People of God know their shepherds, and vice versa. The process of choosing a bishop should, to a large extent, include clergy and laity. Many times in the Roman rite, the process seems opaque and the criteria vague. If the unspoken criterion is "who do you know," and the criterion is hierarchy, the result may be a bishop who doesn't know the people and needs of the diocese.

Human rights and Due Process

Still another major reform involves human rights. The Church recognizes the dignity of the person—all of us are made in the image of God—and should be the conscience of the world in defense of human rights. But the Church can't criticize credibly violations of human rights in governments, while its own transgressions cloud its Gospel witness. Matthew 7 shouts loudly, "remove the wooden beam from your eye first." The Church at every level should have policies and protocols and due processes so that it can be a credible beacon of light for human rights in the wider-world.

One of the great scandals in the Catholic Church is the clergy sexual abuse of minors, and its cover-up by bishops. Many Catholics are scandalized and demoralized by this. People understandably have a hard time reconciling child abuse with Luke 6:36: "Be merciful, just as (also) your Father is merciful." They do not easily forgive predators who have betrayed their vocation to teach, sanctify and pastor the faithful. One bishop said, when announcing a settlement in restitution to several hundred survivors of sexual abuse, "I recognize that the abuse stole so much from you—your childhood, your innocence, your safety, your ability to trust and, in many cases, your faith…The Church let you down, and I'm very sorry."

"Ecclesia semper reformanda" (the Church always reformable) begins with the bishops and priests.

The sex abuse scandal also has compromised the Church's good work in its wide-ranging ministries. One estimate is that dioceses and religious communities have paid out a staggering four billion dollars, money from the pockets from faithful laypersons that could have helped so many worthy ministries.

Where did these settlement monies come from? Often, a combination of cash, proceeds from the sale of land and buildings, and insurance payments. Some dioceses have established compensation funds, with independent reconciliation and reparations programs where administrators evaluate the credibility of each clergy sexual abuse claim and determine compensation in light of such factors as the abuse, the accuser's age and so forth. But the link between "credible claims" and "corroborating evidence" is seldom publicly stated.

Other dioceses have filed for Chapter 11 bankruptcy to protect parish assets, school moneys and trusts and continue ministries. Pending and future lawsuits are settled in bankruptcy courts.

Regrettably, not a few Catholics have reacted to such heinous, sinful crimes by leaving the Church; others are understandably asking, "Why should I stay?" At the very least, they're stating clearly, as one person did in recent news, "I am a Catholic. If there are problems in the Church, I want to hear first from the Church, not from a grand jury."

It became obvious in 2002 that the bishops had to address clergy sexual abuse of minors. When Bernard Law was made archbishop of Boston's 2.1 million Catholics eighteen years earlier, he received a letter from another bishop about a sexual abuse allegation against a priest. Law simply reassigned the priest to another parish. Six parishes and dozens of alleged victims later, the priest was convicted in 2002 on a charge of indecent assault and battery within Massachusetts' criminal statutes of limitations. Two cases of rape were dismissed due to the time limit (criminal and civil statutes vary from state to state).

After arranging a multi-million-dollar settlement for multiple victims, Law resigned and never faced criminal charges. In fact, Pope John Paul II assigned him as archpriest of the papal Basilica of Santa Maria Maggiore in Rome.

Many Catholics were broadsided by these revelations. They also were surprised that episcopal management lacked protective protocols.

At their annual spring meeting in 2002, in Dallas, bishops hurriedly hammered out a series of protocols to govern the handling of sexual abuse, but only by priests and deacons. The bishops astonishingly exempted themselves even though they knew they had sexual predators among their ranks. These protocols became known as the Charter for the Protection of Children and Young People.

The Charter definitely has made a substantial difference. Studies – notably a report from the John Jay College of Criminal Justice — revealed that instances of clergy sex abuse of minors declined precipitously after

2002, so that the reporting of new cases is down to a trickle. Still a trickle is one too many.

As for justice, many argue the so-called Dallas Charter is flawed. It focuses on abuse by priests and deacons and excludes bishops from the protocols of their own Charter. Why should bishops be excluded? Some covered up crimes, and some were alleged abusers themselves. Pope Francis, in the carefully named 2019 church law letter "Vos estis lux mundi" (You are the light of the world), states that bishops and cardinals are not exempt from efforts "to prevent and combat these crimes that betray the trust of the faithful."

More to the point, the "Dallas Charter" is flawed from the viewpoint of American jurisprudence. It's vague on the essential presumption of innocence until proven guilty beyond a reasonable doubt. With the Charter's phrase "semblance of truth" as a determinant of guilt, instead of clear and convincing evidence, it holds clergy to a different standard. Once an allegation is made and publicized, without due process, the accused is presumed guilty.

Last not least, the Charter ultimately undermines vocations to the ministerial priesthood. Thoughtful priestly candidates may have second thoughts about ordination if bishops don't ensure their rights to due process and to a good name (unless proven otherwise) so that the truth of an accusation may be determined.

A case in point is the Pennsylvania Grand Jury Report in 2018. Pennsylvania's attorney general released the report with considerable publicity. Bishops were virtually silent, providing no context and not a word about protocols in place now to safeguard minors and vulnerable adults.

The Pennsylvania report, covering a seventy-year period, identified approximately two percent of the clergy in that period who were "credibly" accused of sexual abuse against minors. Two-thirds of the accused were dead, and many of the allegations weren't proven.

The accused– be they bishop or priest or layperson – and the accuser must have clearly defined rights so that the truth of an accusation may be determined, and justice served. But the word "credible" indicates "not entirely impossible." A "credible" allegation is thus given a semblance of truth and is not found manifestly false or frivolous. What of the standard of clear and convincing evidence. "Guilt by Accusation," to employ the title of legal scholar Alan Dershowitz' cautionary new book, is a threat.

Regarding possible suspension of clergy, a transparent analysis is needed: is the allegation frivolous or is it credible from clear evidence?

Bishops can't do such a task; their "cover ups" prove the point. Competent lay experts can best collaborate to serve the Church in accord with the principles of jurisprudence.

A major problem with the Dallas charter is that the bishops exempted themselves from the protocols. In other words, how deal with bishops who engage in or permit sexual misconduct.

At their June 2019 meeting in Baltimore, the American bishops adopted a policy whereby allegations of sexual misconduct by bishops are referred to the Metropolitan bishop of the region who then oversees the investigation and sends his findings to Rome. The Pope would make a final determination. Lay involvement in the process was optional.

The first case under this new protocol proved how inadequate this protocol is. Michael Bransfield of the diocese of Wheeling—Charleston, West Virginia had been suspended due to multiple allegations of sexual harassment and misuse of diocesan funds. William Lori of Baltimore, metropolitan of the province in which the diocese is located, carried out the investigation and sent the results to Rome. But Lori redacted the report to conceal the names of bishops who had received substantial cash gifts from Bransfield during his tenure at Wheeling—Charleston. Bransfield, it turns out, was not indiscriminate in his pattern of giving. He gave monetary gifts to powerful archbishops, and also to two young priests he allegedly hoped to seduce.

Rather than use money from a diocesan fund to help the needy or support the good works of the diocese, Bransfield used the churchgoers' money to fund a luxurious lifestyle for himself and to give cash gifts to bishops who were in a position to do him favors. The cultivation of favorable relationships through gifts to papal nuncios is noteworthy in that nuncios can influence episcopal appointments.

In Bransfield's case, rumors about his predatory sexual behavior and his questionable financial practices were circulating for at least five years before he abruptly retired in 2018. Yet no action was taken until after he retired.

The question is what to make of this metropolitan plan adopted by the American bishops. Lori investigated Bransfield, yet he tried to protect bishops by deleting their names from the report. He tampered with transparency and accountability. The Washington Post made the original investigative report public.

Metropolitans are not de facto more trustworthy than other bishops. The crux of the objection to the metropolitan plan is that it is essentially a self-policing plan, with no assurance of transparency and accountability. The Church in the United States deserves a better system than the metropolitan plan.

Pope Francis has now abolished the rule of "pontifical secrecy" regarding crimes of violence and abuse: a rule used in past to protect pedophiles and prevent investigation. This new reform will facilitate coordination and communication regarding legitimate legal requests from civil authorities.

The lack of local oversight in the Bransfield case also points to what the federal Sarbanes-Oxley Act of 2002 addressed, regarding auditing and financial regulations for public companies. There was an expectation that private institutions would follow suit, but the Church leaders apparently saw themselves as above such transparency.

The importance of process

A recent case in Australia accentuates the point of jurisprudence: the riveting and controversial "Cathedral trials" of George Pell, former archbishop of Melbourne and former prefect of the Vatican's Secretariat for the Economy. This has the makings of a textbook case. It shows a disregard for evidence.

Although Pell was accused of multiple offenses, most were dismissed, owing to a lack of admissible evidence.

However, in 2018 a magistrate ordered Pell to stand trial for allegedly sexually abusing two choirboys in the sacristy after mass, in 1996 and 1997. One came forward in 2015 to make the allegation against Pell after the other choirboy died of a drug overdose. This second boy had apparently told his mother long before he died that Pell never abused him. The police investigated then but found no evidence. Pell initially stated the allegations were rubbish, but he eventually volunteered to return to Australia to clear his name, even though he could have invoked diplomatic immunity.

In September 2018, a mistrial was declared, after jurors were unable to reach a unanimous verdict; the jury reportedly voted 10-2 to dismiss the charges.

Three months later, in a second trial, Pell was unanimously found guilty.

A range of witnesses had testified that Pell was never alone in the sacristy with altar servers or members of the choir, and that in all the circumstances under allegation, several people would have been present in the room. The sacristy in Melbourne's Cathedral has large open-plan rooms, each with open arches and halls, and multiple entrances and exits. Witnesses testified that Pell was constantly surrounded by other clergy and guests following Sunday masses, and choristers had a room entirely separate from the sacristy in which they gathered as a group.

Observers at the trials questioned whether some tactics used by prosecutors were intended to stoke anti-clerical feelings in jury members.

In March 2019, Pell began a six-year prison term in solitary confinement. That August, the Victoria Court of Appeal upheld the conviction with a split 2-1 decision. In his dissent, Justice Mark Weinberg found the accuser's testimony displayed discrepancies, inadequacies, and lacked probative value. He called the accuser's account of an incident "entirely implausible and quite unconvincing" and found it "impossible to accept." Weinberg wrote of a significant possibility that the cardinal "may not have committed these offenses," so "these convictions cannot be permitted to stand."

Justices Fergusson and Maxwell accepted the one accuser's testimony, without any corroborating evidence, and disregarding other testimony. In other words, guilt was determined on the word of one accuser, not on evidence. And the accuser is anonymous while the accused was publicly vilified. Doesn't the accused have a right to know his accuser *in court*?

In jurisprudence an allegation ought to be determined true or false on the basis of evidence "beyond a reasonable doubt," not whether one witness is found "compelling." The burden of proof rests with the prosecutor/accuser. Fergusson and Maxwell stated the accuser's testimony had the "ring of truth." Surely no court should determine guilt on the basis of "ring of truth" or a "semblance of truth." There was no corroborating physical or circumstantial evidence, only the testimony of one person whose "ring of truth" rang some bells. Pell's application to appeal has been referred to the Australian High Court for decision, probably in spring 2020.

In light of the modern day "MeToo" movement, an accuser's statement may suffice. This is an incredible miscarriage of justice.

Pell had the financial resources of the Church to

pay his legal fees. The Dallas Charter is conspicuously silent about the source of funds if a priest must challenge an allegation. Our faithful parishioners, and our priests, deserve clarity and accountability regarding adjudication and criminal or civil settlements (be they monetary or nonmonetary).

Seminaries

Last, but not least, seminaries or houses of formation call for ongoing reform. One of the most vexing questions today is how to prepare candidates for ministerial priesthood.

The Gospels have an enduring attraction. So too the lives of committed Christians, living and working authentically to share the Good News of Jesus Christ.

Yet we live in a cultural climate of self-interest. Robert Bellah, a distinguished sociologist, described in *Habits of Heart* an ethic of "how to get ahead in the corporate bureaucratic world while maximizing one's private goodies." He identified a time of moving away from older ideals, away from religious man/woman and political man/woman, away from ideals oriented to the common good, the other. Such a challenging culture requires that a priest excel in theology.

Someone asked why is it that "the Catholic priest, carrier of the most fascinating, most amazing, most significant story in the history of humankind is not captivated by it, does not shiver and shake when he thinks of it, does not sweat blood preparing to preach it, rarely preaches with the profound passion of the Protestant pastor, cannot bring his people to laugh with him and weep with him as he retells in a contemporary idiom the perennial parable that is Jesus gloriously alive?"

The Second Vatican Council restated a triple function of priestly ministry: to proclaim the good news, to shepherd the faithful and to celebrate the sacred mysteries. I like this description of the priest: "to continue the service and mission of Jesus Christ as prophet, priest and king and thereby, lead all others in the household of faith to that fullness of service and mission appropriate to their baptismal call."

The priest must be a person of prayer, must take the time – prayer time – to allow God and Christ to call him to mission each day. For the Church is essentially a mission Church. It must go out of itself to the world. The priest is called as Jesus was called, anointed as Jesus was anointed, to be sent as Jesus was to evangelize the world. The priest has to be a flesh-and-blood person in whom parishioners can recognize the transcendent dimension of their own lives. They grapple with important questions: Who is God? Where do they find God? Where does God find them? How can we know God better? How can we sustain our relationship with God? What are the signs that this relationship is real and alive?

Ministry is a privileged place for meeting the living Christ: sick people, dying people, earnest people, struggling people.

There are other places where we find God and where God finds us. We find God in silence and in solitude – – in the solitude of celibacy and the solitude of being a man of God. We find God too in contemplation as we meditate upon the works of God in the human life cycle: from birth through growth, through sin and reconciliation, through friendship and marriage and the giving of life, through work and play, through sickness and health, and eventually death.

The task of preparing candidates for ministerial priesthood is formidable. Priests are called to be many things to many different people. Our liturgies must inspire, our preaching should invite people to deeper faith, and our social ministry ought to meet crucial needs. Moreover, we have to grasp clearly the significance of symbols in our tradition —sacraments, creeds, devotions, fasting – and communicate these effectively.

How do we prepare candidates for this? Two structures are predominant: free standing seminaries; and houses of formation close to graduate theological faculties. My preference is the latter. Free standing seminaries, a product of the sixteenth century Council of Trent, can easily become isolated and breed clericalism: generally, a not easily defined pejorative term.

The point is the Church is the whole people of God, clergy and laity. A lofty or remote clericalism short-circuits that principle. Such clerics might be mistaken for rulers in — as a visitor in Rome put it – a "grand palace."

To bring about the fullness of God's kingdom, Church structures should be comprised of representatives of the whole people of God, dedicated to the mission of evangelizing. The work of the dicasteries, bishops' conferences, diocesan and parish structures is "evangelization so that Christ, the light of nations, may be known and witnessed to in words and deeds, and this

His Body, the Church, may be built up," the draft of Pope Francis's new constitution reads.

Long ago, the twentieth-century Jesuit ecumenist Bernard Leeming captured my thoughts about the search for Christian unity. Leeming said — to paraphrase him — that the very desire for unity, vague though it may be, unfruitful of concrete results though it may seem, should at all costs be clung to. We should not be discouraged by what appears to be our scant progress, for we trust not in our own efforts but in the Almighty God, to whom nothing is impossible. To this God and Father of our Lord Jesus Christ, we offer all our ecumenical efforts and prayers. Through the power of the Holy Spirit, may they help us, the Church, to experience in ever greater measure the unity in love which is already the joyful possession of the "great multitude, which no one could count, from every nation, race, people, and tongue. They stood before the throne and before the Lamb....They cried out in a loud voice: 'Salvation comes from our God, who is seated on the throne, and from the Lamb'" (Revelation 7:9-10).

In sum, we Catholics continually must renew ourselves and our Church, be credible witnesses to the Gospel and let the Spirit of God who breathes where it wills, do his work through the People of God. That's precisely what Pope John XXIII did in his papal ministry. And that's hopefully what another council of the Church will do. The time is ripe for a third Vatican Council.

The night before Jesus died, He implored:

> "I pray not only for them (the disciples),
> but also for those who will believe in me

through their word, so that they may all be one, as you, Father, are in me, and I in you, that they also may be (one) in us, that the world may believe that you sent me. And I have given them the glory you gave me, so that they may be one, as we are one, I in them and you in me, that they may be brought to perfection as one, that the world may know that you sent me, and that you loved them even as you loved me" (John 17:20-23).

INDEX

Vatican documents appear at www.vatican.va

Printed in the United States
By Bookmasters